On the Farm

A Can-You-Find-It Book

PEBBLE
a capstone imprint

Cock-a-Doodle-Doo!

Can you find
these things?

 spider

 ninja

 popcorn

 wooden spoon

ax

cactus

avocado

starfish

lightning bolt

guitar

Spring Planting

Can you find these things?

 seahorse

 hamster

 pitcher

 acorn

 sailboat

 flamingo

 ruler

 stopwatch

 monster

 ice skate

Barn Buddies

Can you find
these things?

sea
turtle

fish

giraffe

butterfly

 hamburger

 nest

 pizza

 spoons

 dragon

 robot

Busy Barnyard

Can you find
these things?

hot
pepper

cardinal

pretzel

helicopter

 lantern

 sand castle

 key

 duck

 Statue of Liberty

 spatula

Duck, Duck, Goose!

Can you find these things?

hot dog

spaceship

lollipop

hat

 clover

 watermelon

 leaf

 ice-cream cone

 truck

 deer

Playful Pigpen

Can you find these things?

safety pin   eel   hair dryer   hippo

 flashlight sandwich shark pastry tractor cake

Tractor Time

Can you find
these things?

bluebird

dog

thumbtack

duckling

milk
jug

cupid

rose

diploma

shoe

candy
cane

Horses and Hay

Can you find these things?

fudge roll

panda

taco

mouse

 basketball

 toaster

 fox

 police car

 rooster

 boot

A for Apple

Can you find these things?

train

mousetrap

trophy

pencil

 strawberry   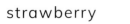 glasses   wagon   penguin   violin   robin

Happy Harvest

Can you find these things?

motorcycle

bubble gum

arrow

Christmas tree

crab

dinosaur

dump
truck

mermaid

grapes

bus

Fall Festival Fun

Can you find these things?

 kangaroo

 camera

 spray bottle

 cherries

camel

squirrel

golf
clubs

puppy

gumball
machine

fire
hydrant

Goodnight, Farm!

Can you find these things?

hanger

ghost

plum

bull

 poodle

 scissors

 record

 candle

 tiger

 tuba

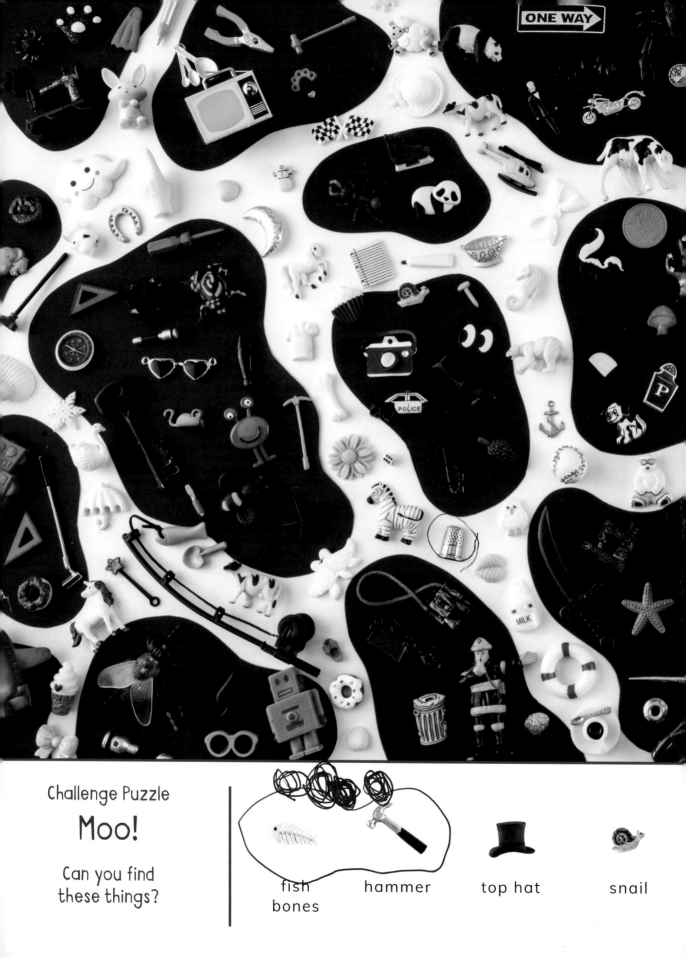

ONE WAY

POLICE

MILK

P

Challenge Puzzle

Moo!

Can you find
these things?

fish
bones

hammer

top hat

snail

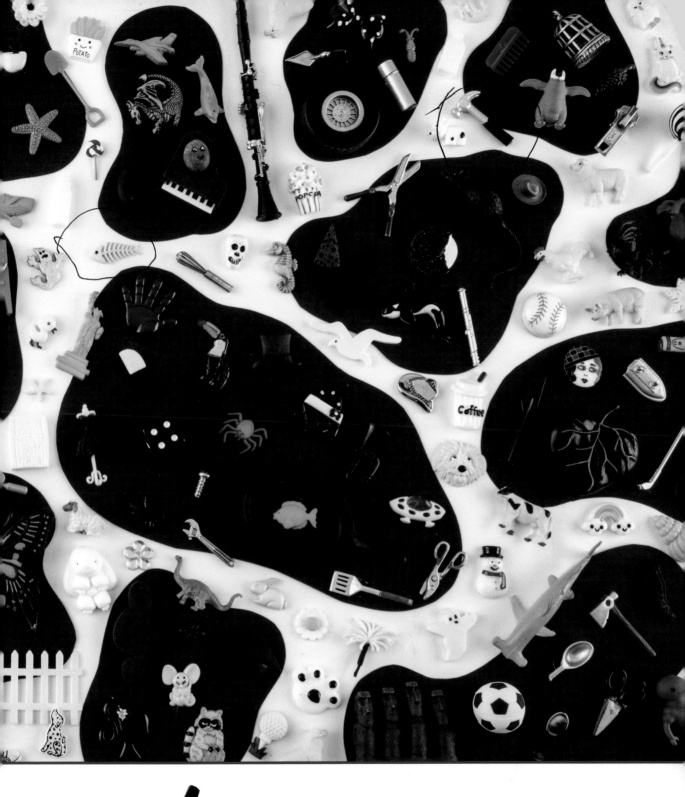

 compass oar thimble wand trumpet horseshoe

Moo!: Answer Key

Psst! Did you know that Pebs the Pebble was hiding
in EVERY PUZZLE in this book?

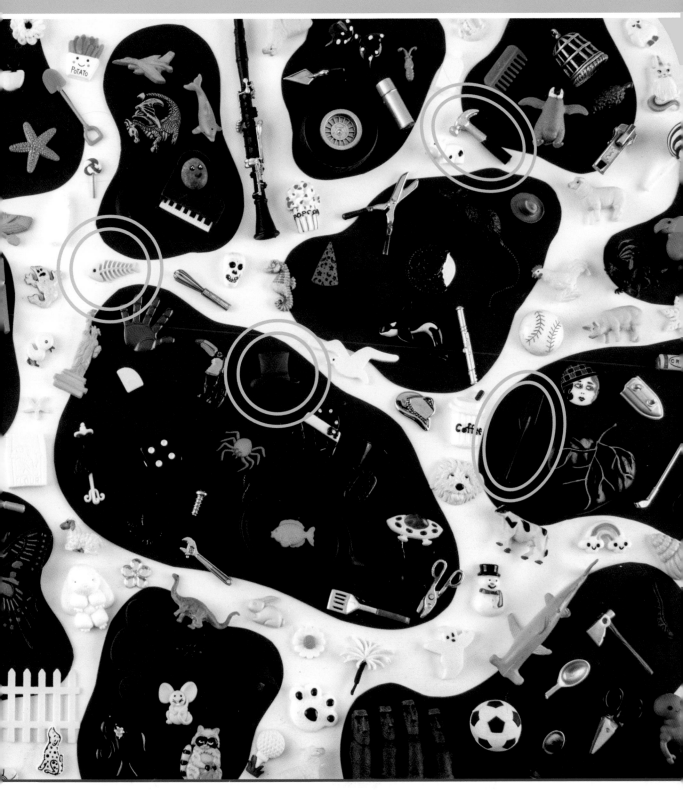

It's true! Go back and look! Hi.

Look for other books in this series:

The author dedicates this book to her favorite farmers, Arnold and Eileen Nokleby.

Pebble Sprout is published by Pebble, an imprint of Capstone.
1710 Roe Crest Drive, North Mankato, Minnesota 56003
www.capstonepub.com

Copyright © 2021 by Capstone. All rights reserved. No part of this publication may be reproduced in whole or in part, or stored in a retrieval system, or transmitted in any form or by any means, electronic, mechanical, photocopying, recording, or otherwise, without written permission of the publisher.

Library of Congress Cataloging-in-Publication Data
Names: Thompson, Heidi E., author.
Title: On the farm : a can-you-find-it book / Heidi E. Thompson.
Description: North Mankato, Minnesota : Pebble, an imprint of Capstone, [2021] | Series: Can you find it? | Audience: Ages 6-8 | Audience: Grades K-1 | Summary: "Treat kids to a seek-and-find field trip to the farm. Kids will discover the different animals, machines, and buildings found on a farm in these full-color photo puzzles. Pictographs and word labels are included in each to-find list"— Provided by publisher.
Identifiers: LCCN 2020031013 (print) | LCCN 2020031014 (ebook) | ISBN 9781977132123 (hardcover) | ISBN 9781977133144 (paperback) | ISBN 9781977154705 (ebook)
Subjects: LCSH: Farms—Juvenile literature. | Picture puzzles—Juvenile literature.
Classification: LCC S519 .T49 2021 (print) | LCC S519 (ebook) | DDC 630—dc23
LC record available at https://lccn.loc.gov/2020031013
LC ebook record available at https://lccn.loc.gov/2020031014

Image Credits: All photos by Capstone Studio/Karon Dubke

Editorial Credits: Jill Kalz, editor; Karon Dubke, Marcy Morin, and Heidi Thompson, set stylists; Kathy McColley, production specialist